McKayla DeBonis

# Semicolon

;

Semicolon ;

*Semicolon*
*;*

*Copyright © 2017 McKayla DeBonis*

*All rights reserved. This book or any portion thereof may not be reproduced or used in any manner whatsoever without the express written permission of the author except for the use of brief quotations in book review.*

*Art cover by Caloua Zhane*

*Page art by Rachel Aquino*

*Edited by Cheyenne Raine*

*ISBN: 978-1978328365*

McKayla DeBonis

*To*
My mother, for molding & building me up
into a strong women.
I love you to the moon & back

Semicolon ;

Dear Reader,

I spilled my heart into this, shining my light
on all the poison that was invading my life.
Through it all, I have learned there is so
much to live for.
I promise that what you're feeling will pass
& that you're stronger than you believe.

Poems are untitled
because you're in control of your own story.

Always,
McKayla

McKayla DeBonis

<u>Trigger Warnings Include:</u>

- Descriptions of Anxiety
- Descriptions of Panic Attacks
- Sexual Abuse / Harassment
  - Depression
  - Suicidal Tendencies
  - Self Harm
  - Body Dysmorphia
- Natural Disaster References

Semicolon ;

*Darkness;*

McKayla DeBonis

i live in the well hidden shadows where
darkness envelopes me with a welcome hand
    no one sees me
     & no one knows my name

      - *except the shadows that lurk in the dark*

Semicolon ;

here i am
      lying
      broken
      &
      naked on the ground

            - *untouchable, even by your hands*

McKayla DeBonis

every day riptides grasp at my ankles

threatening to sweep me under harsh crashing waves

> - *maybe i'll let them*

Semicolon ;

it's revolting
sticks
&
bones
*"you're wasting away"*
*"eat more"*
*"what a little bird"*
mocking words whispered in my ear

- *i wanted a different skin to call home*

## McKayla DeBonis

i wanted to feel something more than the
*hollowness* that was
    *e t c h i n g*
itself inside my body

# Semicolon ;

you
*smothered*
me

depriving me of
*oxygen*

> *- leaving me to die*

McKayla DeBonis

i can't locate my voice
my heart is pounding at a frantic tempo
          **deep**
            *b r e a t h s*
i try so hard to push away the anxious
feelings
&
shove them in a dark closet
to lock them away

                        - *& throw away the key*

Semicolon ;

>
> groundings trembled
> as the floor fell out
> sweeping my lungs away
> & leaving an ache for breath
> *gasping —*
> this is the consequence when the
> bottom falls out
>
> - *to lungs that give way*

McKayla DeBonis

i was a wrecking ball for destruction
how could i reduce the casualties?
the destruction of myself would come first

- *because the force of forgetting you
became unbearable*

Semicolon ;

you came
you *conquered*

*destroying*

*everything*

- *i lost a chunk of my soul that day*

## McKayla DeBonis

sadness clings to my drying skin
leaving me stagnant
&
*c o l d*
to the core

i
*a c h e*
for the feeling of your
*w a r m t h*

                 - *but i know it'll never come*

Semicolon ;

**you** told me that i was a storm
    *twisting*
havoc in your heart
**are** you ready to
    *break?*
because you told me **the** pain isn't worth
your
    *effort*
but a **storm** is
    *beautiful*
is that **not** what you once said?
i guess all are
except **me**

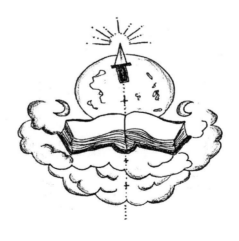

McKayla DeBonis

sickly pale lines etched in all directions
forever a visible past

- *sealed forever in the tomb of my skin*

# Semicolon ;

you ripped my heart & soul wide open
left it bare for anyone to touch
you stripped me to my skeleton
left me bare for all to see & mock
how can i recover when all who see me
stare right through me?
you laid me bare

        - *& didn't bother to cover me up*

## McKayla DeBonis

**i'd** search for you in everyone i met even though you've
      **been** gone for far too long now
        you left me **dead** in the dirt
   **only** because you couldn't handle me
   **an** even then you wouldn't spare the
     **hour** it would take to find me
so why am i stuck in this *limbo* searching for you?

Semicolon ;

i've said it so many times
over & over
screamed it into my pillow late at night
but each time my mouth cannot form the words
i cannot push the sound off my tongue
it dies inside my throat
i've said goodbye to you so many times

- *you just never heard me say it*

## McKayla DeBonis

i
abandoned
myself
in
my darkest
moment

Semicolon ;

you are still a tornado that rips the
foundation from underneath me
i'm trying to find shelter in his arms
but you keep coming back

- *tearing everything away*

# McKayla DeBonis

i choked on all the pain that came rushing in
i buried everything so long ago
&
yet it still lurks at the surface
but you didn't care if all this pain

- *left me hollow*

Semicolon ;

even though my skin will shed your touch in
3 weeks
&
my lips will have met another

 my heart will still race at the
*sound*
of your name

even though my body will forget you
you've become a stain that i can't
*erase*

McKayla DeBonis

missing you
is pouring salt on an open wound

- *& yet i do it still*

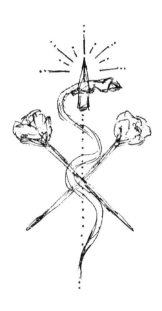

Semicolon ;

i struggle so hard to love myself
& every
single
flaw

## McKayla DeBonis

i break
loathing myself
as i drag teeth across my skin
relishing in bliss as red rivers flow
i give in
only to feel

n u m b

with ease i am elated when serrated teeth dig
miles into my skin

- *ripping slowly apart*

# Semicolon ;

10.
i forgot how to breathe
9.
he robbed me of happiness
8.
that sank me lower into my grave
7.
do you feel dirty yet?
6.
don't forget to embalm my heart
5.
i forget how to feel
4.
you make me numb
3.
this isn't healthy
2.
so how can i escape from you?
1.
& still remember how to breathe backwards from ten?

## McKayla DeBonis

i let the water turn my skin an angry shade
as i shift in endless thoughts
losing myself in the steam
*blistering*
the pain is physical

                         - *not just in my head*

## Semicolon ;

it was easier loving you at arms

l e n g t h

instead of letting you get too

close
to my heart

## McKayla DeBonis

i folded each edge seamlessly
carefully crafting my points
hiding myself away from the world

- *in perfect creases*

# Semicolon ;

until —
you untraced those creases
*u n ∂ o i n g me*
like an unfolding origami in the palm of your hand

McKayla DeBonis

the darkness at the base of my brain
*whispers*
i dismiss it
but it's still there
waiting for another chance

- *to break me*

# Semicolon ;

you left a hole in my heart
it was so long ago

- *but it's still there*

McKayla DeBonis

it comes back ripping through you
*unforgiving*
a darkness that can devour you whole

- *touching the depths of your soul*

Semicolon ;


we spilled our secrets in a parked car
&
even when you left
i kept yours safe from prying eyes

- *but you didn't return the gesture*

McKayla DeBonis

static in my ears
as blood swirls down the drain
an equal intensity magnifying in my chest
*burning*
as the world fades out

     -  *& all that's left is white noise*
         -  *anxiety wins*

Semicolon ;

it was *suffocating*
the way you put out your cigarette ash in my veins

- *a circulating darkness*

McKayla DeBonis

on the night you offered me your wing
  i almost let myself slip through your grasp
    finally taking darkness as
      my husband

        *forever*
      *even in death*

                    - *suicide*

Semicolon ;

i am
the face of my own *death*
slowly ripping at the seams

        -  *until i fall apart completely*

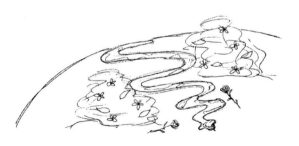

McKayla DeBonis

dear me

i don't see you making it to 18
i don't see you fulfilling your dreams
i don't see you marrying the love of your life
or having the kids you want

all i see is darkness
it stretches for miles
blocking everything that lies in your path

it's a cancer
eating away at you
leaving holes in everything good

where is the light you so desperately seek?
she slipped through your grasp

all that's left is a never ending darkness
swallowing you whole

- *a suicide note from my 14 year old self*

Semicolon ;

i'm begging you

- *tell me how i can heal from this*

McKayla DeBonis

*Light;*

Semicolon ;


        i am the *light* in my *darkness*

McKayla DeBonis

when your scars begin to heal
&
the smoke finally clears
you tell yourself
*"this time will be different"*
it's a promise to be better
to go forward instead of backward —
    happy sobriety birthday

       - *3 years*

## Semicolon ;

after us
relearning happiness seemed so impossible
for someone so broken
but i continued to fight just so i could have
the last *laugh*

McKayla DeBonis

delicate love is the only thing that can be
found here

                         - *if you want it*

Semicolon ;

night skies remind me of the stardust
sprinkled upon your face
&
the rivers that ran down your naked face
as you conquered my heart with grace

- *smoothing mountains in your wake*

## McKayla DeBonis

surviving my sadness was never easy
it came in *waves*
even when i thought it was safe

>   - *but i am living proof those waves will pass*

Semicolon ;

i will rise from the ashes
stronger than before
bolder
&
brand new

- *you will not be my demise*

McKayla DeBonis

i am the sun
& moon of my own damn universe

# Semicolon ;

you're so beautiful
i'm sorry that i've harmed you time
& time again
it has taken me so long to love every inch of
you
i was blind
even to all the beauty you possess
i missed it
but i see it clear as day now
you're so beautiful

- *a love letter to my body*

McKayla DeBonis

rising to the morning air
as the sun winked out —
like a breath held
was released to gold

## Semicolon ;

i caressed every inch of myself
loving every fault my fingers found
i fell in love with my chocolate eyes because
who cares if they're not blue like the ocean
my mind is beautiful and full of life
i fell back in love with the person i'm
becoming

before letting another back into my heart

reveling the way a naked face looks in the
mirror
&
embracing the rawness of it all

i'm falling back in love with the big heart
inside my chest

- *loving myself all over again as if it's
brand new*

McKayla DeBonis

clouds will disperse
&
the sky will open up again as the storm passes
&
you will find yourself once more
because it is only the *beginning*

Semicolon ;

 

you stayed because you were afraid the
lantern in my heart would fade
but once you left
it swallowed my heart whole

i never needed you to *shine*

McKayla DeBonis

*let
go*

Semicolon ;

i planted self love in the chambers of my
heart
strings connecting every inch
it was solemn
yet full of so much *light*

- *& promise of tomorrow*

McKayla DeBonis

my soul is eternal
my heart is everlasting
my words are fluent

i am a masterpiece

- *that i alone have created*

Semicolon ;

i discovered myself in the night
as my *light* burned over the stars

## McKayla DeBonis

there is electricity when we touch
a fire that burns so deep
i'm scared one day it'll swallow me whole
maybe that's not so bad
to be engulfed so deeply in a love that burns
brighter than the sun
as you turn my skies to lilac

- *to a lover*

Semicolon ;

take care of your heart
take care of your soul
take care of your mind

- ***mental health*** *is important*

## McKayla DeBonis

dear me

things will work out
this pain won't last forever and you'll see the
*light* again
& when you feel panic bubble in your chest
remember to breathe
this is *temporary*
it won't last
&
i promise the suffocation of sadness will pass
just keep fighting
keep swinging
because even through all of your *darkness*
you'll find your *light*

Semicolon ;

& for the first time in my life

i didn't know despair

- *i knew hope*

McKayla DeBonis

Acknowledgements:

I want all my readers to feel safe and if you are in need of help, please reach out because someone is there to help you.
You are not alone.

**National Suicide Prevention Lifeline**
800-273-8255

**Samaritans (UK Crisis Help, Anywhere in the UK or Ireland)**
116 123

**National Youth Crisis Hotline**
(800) 442-4673

**IMAlive — imalive.org**

**National Domestic Violence Hotline**
(800) 799-7233

**Eating Disorder Awareness and Prevention**
(800) 931-2237

**Rape, Abuse, and Incest National Network (RAINN)**
(800) 656-4673

**National Domestic Violence/Child Abuse/Sexual Abuse**
(800) 799-7233

# Semicolon ;

Page art done by Rachel Aquino:

- Connect with her on instagram @Rach.lazatin

- Connect with her on twitter @rachellazatinnn

Cover Art done by Caloua Zhane

- Her Business Email: calouazhane@yahoo.com

Edited by Cheyenne Raine

- Connect with her on instagram @rainepoetry

- Connect with her on twitter @rainepoetry

- Or on her website: rainepoetry.com

# McKayla DeBonis

### About the Author

Mckayladebonis.com
Twitter / Instagram: @mckayladebonis
Bookstagram: @accio.__.hogwartz

The author of,
    Semicolon; and Bones in the Garden.

McKayla is also working on her debut young adult fiction novel! She is a bookworm of a soul, and realized that her mind was spinning with the same creativity of her beloved writers, leading to her own poetry, prose, and other writings. Her Hogwarts house is Hufflepuff and you'll definitely find her with a cup of coffee in her hand and her nose in a book at all times.

Made in the USA
Lexington, KY
03 February 2018